James McKellar Bugbee

Russia and Turkey

The Eastern question, historically considered

James McKellar Bugbee

Russia and Turkey
The Eastern question, historically considered

ISBN/EAN: 9783337299330

Printed in Europe, USA, Canada, Australia, Japan

Cover: Foto ©ninafisch / pixelio.de

More available books at **www.hansebooks.com**

THE

EASTERN QUESTION,

HISTORICALLY CONSIDERED;

WITH NOTES ON THE RESOURCES OF RUSSIA AND TURKEY,
AND AN ABSTRACT OF THEIR TREATIES
WITH THE UNITED STATES.

By JAMES M. BUGBEE.

𝕎𝕚𝕥𝕙 𝕄𝕒𝕡𝕤.

BOSTON:

JAMES R. OSGOOD AND COMPANY,
(Late Ticknor & Fields, and Fields, Osgood, & Co.)
· 1877.

CONTENTS.

HISTORICAL STATEMENT

OF THE

EASTERN QUESTION,

ESPECIALLY OF THE

CAUSES WHICH LED TO THE PRESENT WAR.

———————•♦•———————

THE desire of the Russians to obtain possession of Constantinople is said to be as old as
Russian nationality, and is founded on the idea
that the Tsars — as the successors of the Byzantine
rulers, and the descendants of Cæsar Augustus —
ought to rule in the Holy City on the Bosphorus,
in place of the infidels who hold in cruel bond-
age their brothers of the Slavonic race and of
the Orthodox Church. "The position of the Russian Christians under the Tartar domination," says
Mr. Wallace, in his recent work on Russia, "was
very like the present position of the Christians in
Turkey. For some time after the conquest, Rus-

sia was ruled as Bulgaria is now; then she
obtained autonomy similar to that of Servia and
Roumania at the present day; and ultimately she
gained complete independence. Thus the Russians long formed the vanguard in the cause of
Slavonic emancipation. They were the first of
the Slavonic people to fall under the Tartar yoke,
and the first to emancipate themselves. This
they have not forgotten; and we cannot wonder
that they should now sympathize with those cog-
nate races which are striving to follow their
example. The epigrammatic saying, that the
sympathy of the Russian people with the Servians and Bulgarians is mere 'philological sentiment,' cannot be accepted by any one who knows
the history of Eastern Europe."

Alison, the historian of Modern Europe, says,
" Encamped for four centuries in Europe, the
Turks have deviated in no respect from the man-
ners and customs of their Asiatic forefathers.[1]

[1] This statement is subject to some modification at the present
day. The Turks have re-organized their military establishment in
accordance with modern ideas, and have, within the present year,
assembled representatives of the people in a legislative body.

Although, from the day that the cannon of Mohammed the Second opened the breach in the walls of Constantinople, — which still exists, to attest the fall of the Emperor of the East, — they have been undisputed masters of the fairest and richest dominion upon earth; yet the great body of them still retain the primitive customs and habits which they brought with them from the mountains of Koordistan. They have in no degree either shared in the improvement, or adopted the manners, or acquired the knowledge, of their European neighbors. Notwithstanding their close proximity to, and constant intercourse with, the democratic commercial communities of Modern Europe, they are yet the devout followers of Mohammed: notwithstanding that they everywhere admit that the star of the crescent is waning before that of the cross, they still adhere in all their institutions to the precepts of the Koran. They rely with implicit faith on the aid of the Prophet, although they are well aware that the followers of Christ are ultimately to expel them from Europe; and themselves point to the gate by which the Muscovite battalions are to enter when they place the cross upon the dome of St. Sophia."

The Eastern question first rose into European importance in the reign of Catherine II., who formed the project of resuscitating the Byzantine Empire. It is a remarkable fact that the position now taken by the Russian Government with regard to the oppressive and barbarous acts of the Turkish Government finds its counterpart, to some extent, in the position taken by the Ottoman power in the time of Catherine. In 1768 the Turks interfered to check the designs of Russia upon Poland by taking arms in support of the liberties and independence of the Poles. In the present instance, Russia interferes to preserve the autonomy of the tributary States of the Turkish Empire, and to protect the religious liberties and independence of the Christian subjects of the Porte.

The interference of the Turks in the first instance was attended by the most disastrous consequences. They showed themselves unequal to the science of modern warfare; their armies and navies were destroyed; and Russian forbearance alone prevented the fall of Constantinople. In giving up the contest, the Turkish ruler said, " Seeing our troops will no longer fight the Russians, it is necessary to conclude peace." By the treaty which followed, the Russians obtained the free navigation of all the Turkish seas, a passage through the Dardanelles, and the establishment of Russian consuls in the Turkish seaports.

In 1787, the Turks, taking alarm at the visit of Catherine to the Crimea, and her personal conference with the Emperor of Germany, rushed into another war, in which they were reduced to such an extent, that Great Britain and Prussia considered it necessary for their own future welfare to check the progress of the Russian power. " Mr. Pitt," says Alison, " put a bridle on the Tsar, and, in conjunction with Prussia, arrested the march of the united Muscovite and Austrian armies when on the high road to Constantinople." Then was established the policy which has since governed the British councils, — the maintenance of the Ottoman power, — a policy which has greatly increased in importance with the extension of the British Empire in India.

It is not necessary to refer, except in the brief-
est manner, to the combinations which were made,
and to the contests which took place, during the
interval between the peace of 1791 (by which
Russia was allowed to retain a large portion of
the territory which she had conquered) and the
Crimean war, as the policy then adopted was
always adhered to ; but there were times when it
became necessary to curb the Turks as well as
to protect them.

In the closing years of the eighteenth century,
the Turks acted in concert with England and
Russia in opposing the French power; but, subsequently, Napoleon obtained the ascendency in the
councils of the divan, and drew the Turks to his
support.   But in 1807 he treacherously deserted
them.   By the secret articles of the Treaty of
Tilsit, it was stipulated, that, in certain contin-
gencies, France and Russia would unite their
efforts "to wrest from the vexations and oppression of the Turkish Empire all its provinces in
Europe, Roumelia and Constantinople alone ex-
cepted."   In the beginning of 1810 Moldavia
and Wallachia were annexed to Russia; and

the Danube, from the Austrian frontier to the sea, was declared to be the southern European boundary of that empire. During the ensuing two years, Russia prosecuted the war against Turkey with vigor and success. But in 1812 she found it necessary to gather all her forces for the impending conflict with Napoleon. Peace was made with Turkey; and the Pruth, instead of the Danube, was agreed upon as the boundary between the two nations. "Made aware," said Napoleon, "by my enemies, of the stipulations of Erfurth, and by Austria of the project for the partition of Turkey, which I had proposed to her, the Turks abandoned themselves, without reserve, to the counsels of England. The British ambassador soon resumed all his former credit with the divan."

The Servians, who had rebelled in 1806, and captured Belgrade, became subject again to the Turkish power after the treaty of 1812; but in 1815 they obtained the right of local self-government.

In 1821 the Greeks rebelled against Turkish rule; and their independence was acknowledged

by the Porte in 1829. The barbarities practised
by the Turks in their efforts to suppress this
rebellion excited the indignation and horror of
civilized nations. The Turkish Government re-
pudiated the efforts of the other European
powers to negotiate in behalf of the Greeks,
and in so doing placed itself on the platform
adopted by the Congress of Laybach in 1821,
that " Almighty Wisdom, in dividing the universe
into different countries, has assigned to each a
sovereign, into whose hands the reins of absolute
authority over the nations subject to his dominion are placed." This is the principle upon
which the sovereign powers of Europe have
always acted. They can ignore it in the case
of Turkey, only by assuming, that as an alien
in blood, language, and religion, she is to be
dealt with in an exceptional manner. The ex-
asperated state of the public feeling against
Turkey on account of the Greek war is shown
in the battle of Navarino, — that "untoward
event," as the Duke of Wellington described it.
The commanders of the allied naval forces in
the Mediterranean (those of England, France,

and Russia) entered the port of Navarino, where
the Turkish fleet was anchored; and, although
war had not been declared, placed their ships
in such a position as to make a collision almost
inevitable. They succeeded in tempting the
Turks into firing the first shot, and then retali-
ated by destroying their fleet of a hundred and
thirty vessels. It was a frightful retaliation;
but, after the excesses of the Turks, it was
hailed with satisfaction by the civilized world.

In 1832 the Egyptians rebelled against Turkish rule, and, under the lead of Ibrahim Pacha,
had such success, that the very existence of the
Turkish Government in Europe was threatened.
The Porte appealed to England first for aid;
and the refusal to respond to that appeal has
been a lasting subject of reproach for the short-
sightedness of the party then in power. In its
extremity, the Porte applied to Russia; and that
power seized the opportunity which its compli-
ance afforded to obtain an ascendency over the
Turkish councils. Out of this grew the treaty
of Unkiar Skelessi, which has occupied a large
space in the politics of Europe. It was provided

that there should be an alliance, offensive and defensive, between the two powers, in pursuance of which Russia agreed to put all her fleets at the disposal of the Porte. This was the substance of the public treaty; but there was a secret article, which provided that the "Ottoman Porte should be bound, in virtue of its obligations toward Russia, to close the Straits of the Dardanelles; that is to say, not to permit any ship-of-war of other foreign powers to enter these straits under any pretence whatever." In 1838 Great Britain made a treaty of commerce with Turkey, which gave it all the advantages accorded to the most favored nations, and opened the Dardanelles and the Black Sea to her commercial vessels.

In 1839 hostilities broke out again between the Turks and the Egyptians; and the successes of the latter again threatened the overthrow of Turkish rule in Europe. The British Government was wise enough, on this occasion, to see the necessity of making the question one in which all the great powers of Europe had an interest. Under the lead of Great Britain, Russia, Austria, and Prussia entered, with that power, into an engagement to maintain the territorial integrity of Turkey. The naval power of England humbled the Egyptian pretensions; and a settlement followed, by which Egypt became a tributary of the Ottoman power. A new treaty was made between Turkey, the Allied Powers, and France, by which the affairs of the East were regulated until the breaking-out of the great war of 1854. By that treaty, the Straits of the Bosphorus and the Dardanelles were " to remain permanently closed against all foreign vessels-of-war as long as the Ottoman Porte shall enjoy peace."

We now come to the period of the Crimean war. Some account of the immediate causes which led to that war, and the results which the war accomplished, or, rather, what it failed to accomplish, are necessary to a proper understanding of the present condition of affairs.

In 1849 Russia and Austria made a demand upon the Porte for the rendition of Kossuth, and other Hungarian and Polish refugees, who had sought an asylum on Turkish soil. The demand was resisted; and the attitude then assumed by

Turkey as a defender of freedom went a long way · towards securing sympathy and support, especially among the English people, at a later day, and when the Turks were threatened on other grounds.

In 1850 the French president, Louis Napoleon, with a view, it is supposed, of diverting the attention of his people from their domestic concerns, began "in cold blood" to agitate the long-forgotten question of the rights belonging to the Latin churches in the control and usufruct of the holy places at Palestine, of which the Turks were the owners.   The Russian Government hastened to support the claims of the Orthodox Church, of which it is the head.   The Turks appear to have been indifferent as to the rival claims of the Greek and Latin churches, and were anxious only to adjust matters so as to satisfy the champions of both ; that is, France and Russia.

"A crowd of monks with bare foreheads stood quarrelling for a key, at the sunny gates of a church in Palestine ; but beyond and above, towering high in the misty North, men saw the ambition of the Tsars."[1]

[1] Kinglake's Invasion of the Crimea.

The difference about the holy places might have been settled without recourse to arms ; but, before its adjustment, it became complicated, by Russian diplomacy, with another question ; namely, the form of a guaranty of rights and immunities to the Christian churches in Turkey. Under this the Emperor Nicholas appears to have had in view a Russian protectorate over the entire Greek Church in the empire of his southern neighbor.

In January, 1853, the emperor, in an interview with the British envoy at St. Petersburg, said, " You know the dreams and plans in which the Empress Catherine was in the habit of indulging : these were handed down to our time. But, while I inherited immense territorial possessions, I did not inherit those visions, — those intentions, if you like to call them so : on the contrary, my country is so vast, so happily circumstanced in every way, that it would be unreasonable in me to desire more territory or more power than I possess: on the contrary, I am the first to tell you, that our great, perhaps our only danger, is that which would arise from an extension given to an empire already too large." He then went on to say that Turkey had fallen into such a state of decrepitude, that, eager as they were for the prolonged existence of the "man," he might suddenly die on their hands. "We cannot," he said, "resuscitate what is dead: if the Turkish Empire falls, it falls to rise no more; and I put it to you, therefore, whether it is not better to be provided beforehand for a contingency than to incur the chaos, confusion, and certainty of a European war, — all of which must attend the catastrophe, if it should occur unexpectedly, and before some ulterior system has been sketched."

Subsequently the emperor sent for the British envoy, and, after some preliminary conversation as to the disposal of the sick man's estate, divulged his scheme, as follows: "The principalities [formerly Moldavia and Wallachia, now Roumania] are, in fact, an independent state, under my protection. This might so continue. Servia might receive the same form of government. So, again, with Bulgaria: there seems to be no reason why this province should not form an independent state. As to Egypt, I quite understand the importance to England of that territory. I can then only say, that if, in the event of a distribution of the Ottoman succession upon the fall of the empire, you should take possession of Egypt, I shall have no objection to offer. I would say the same thing of Candia: that island might suit you; and I do not see why it should not become an English possession."

The British representative gave no encouragement to the proposition; and the Tsar, baffled in that direction, pressed his demand for an engagement, on the part of the Porte, " to secure forever to the Orthodox Church and its clergy all the rights and immunities which they had already enjoyed, and those of which they were possessed from ancient times." The Turkish council refused to enter into any such engagement; and diplomatic intercourse between the two powers was suspended on the last of May, 1853.

The change of the issue, which had been brought about for the aggrandizement of Russia, made it for the interest of France to join England, Austria, and Prussia in giving a qualified support to the Porte in resisting the Russian

demands. On the 9th of April, 1854, the representatives of the four powers above named, in
conference at Vienna, adopted a protocol, in
which they declared, that, in that solemn moment,
their governments remained united in the double
object of maintaining the territorial integrity of
the Ottoman Empire, and of consolidating, in an
interest so much in conformity with the sentiments
of the Sultan, and by every means compatible
with his independence and sovereignty, the civil
and religious rights of the Christian subjects of
the Porte.

The Russians had entered Moldavia on the 2d
of July, 1853, but did not declare war until the
1st of November following. The Sultan, with
the consent of the four powers, had declared war
on the 5th of October, 1853. On the 10th of
April, 1854, the day after the adoption of the
Vienna protocol, a treaty of alliance was formed
between France and England. It is unnecessary
for the purposes of this work to give an account
of the operations of the allied forces. The results of the contest are disclosed in the Treaty
of Paris, which was ratified on the 27th of April,

1856. Great Britain, Austria, France, Russia, and Sardinia declared the Sublime Porte admitted to participate in the advantages of the public law and system (*concert*) of Europe ; they engaged to respect the independence of the Ottoman Empire, and guaranteed in common the strict observance of that engagement; and they declared that they would, in consequence, consider any act tending to its violation as a question of general interest. The ancient rule of the Turkish Empire — prohibiting ships-of-war of foreign powers from entering the Straits of the Dardanelles and the Bosphorus, so long as the Porte is at peace — was re-established. The Black Sea was neutralized : its waters and its ports were thrown open to the mercantile marine of every nation : but the flag-of-war, either of the powers possessing its coasts (except as stipulated in an appended convention between Russia and Turkey), or of any other power, was " formally and in perpetuity interdicted."

Reciting the fact that the Sultan had issued a firman ameliorating the condition of his subjects without distinction of religion or race, and had communicated the same to the contracting parties, the treaty states, that "it is clearly understood that it cannot, in any case, give to the said powers the right to interfere, either collectively or separately, in the relations of His Majesty the Sultan with his subjects, nor in the internal administration of his empire."

It was provided that the principalities of Wallachia and Moldavia should continue to enjoy, under the sovereignty of the Porte and "under the guaranty of the contracting powers," acting collectively, the privileges and immunities of which they were then possessed. The Porte engaged to preserve to the principalities and to Servia their independent and national administration, as well as full liberty of worship, of legislation, of commerce, and of navigation.

Great Britain, France, and Austria entered into a special engagement at the same time, in which they jointly and severally guaranteed the independence and integrity of the Ottoman Empire, and declared that any infraction of the stipulations of the Treaty of Paris would be considered by them as a *casus belli.*

The reforms promised by the Sultan, and communicated to the treaty-powers, guaranteed to all Ottoman subjects alike, 1, equality before the law; 2, religious liberty; 3, justice without sale, denial, or delay; 4, local autonomy; 5, security from oppressive taxation. Under the authority of a firman issued by the Sultan on the 12th November, 1861, the principalities of Wallachia and Moldavia were united under the name of Roumania.

Before proceeding to give an account of the acts immediately preceding the present war, it may be well to advert briefly to the failure of the Turkish Government to carry out the reforms which it has from time to time promised and promulgated. Turkey in Europe contains a population of 8,315,000, of which only 1,000,000 are Turks, or Ottomans; the rest are, — Slavonians, of which the estimated number is 4,000,000; Greeks, 900,000; Armenians, 200,000; Jews, 70,000; Albanians, 820,000; Tartars, 11,000; and Gypsies, 214,000. This statement does not include the tributary states of Roumania and Servia, which contain a population of about 5,000,000, nearly all being of the Slavonian race, and of the Christian Church. The religious divisions of the population in the immediate possessions are as follows : Christians, about 4,500,000 ; Mahometans, 3,500,000 ; Israelites, 75,000. It thus appears, that out of a population of about 13,000,000, including the tributary states, only 3,500,000 are of the Mahometan faith, and they form the governing class.

" How is it," says Mr. Godkin,[1] "that so small a body of men, not forming a military organization, not acting, or prepared to act, in concert, scattered over the country in towns and villages like the others, are able to impose on this enormous majority, and maintain a *régime* of crushing oppression and inequality? . . . The reason is to be found in the character of the population no less than in that of the Turks; and there could hardly be a more valuable illustration than this failure affords of the difficulty of making any valuable political change where the bulk of the people are wanting in the courage, ambition, and

[1] The Eastern Question : North American Review, January, 1877.

self-confidence needed to carry it out. The con-
cessions of the Ottoman Government to its Christian subjects have amounted to nothing; first,
because the official class at Constantinople, which
really made them, and which is the class with
which European diplomatists deal, does not represent, and is not in real harmony with, the Mussulman population of the interior, and is utterly
unable to impose its will upon it; and, secondly,
because four centuries of oppression have so
broken the spirit of the Christians, and destroyed
their combativeness, that they are incapable of
using their legal rights as against the conquering
race."

In this connection, an extract from a communi-
cation to Midhat Pacha, the president of the
Turkish council of ministers, who was laboring to
reform the government by establishing a constitution and a national assembly, will be of interest.
This is understood to represent the views of
the average Mussulman; and its authenticity is
vouched for by the American minister at Constantinople.

"At the council, when the constitution and the

national assembly were proposed, Zia Bey thought to support the proposition by quoting a passage from the Koran: 'Do no evil, but always seek the good.'

"It is but proper, we think, to substitute for that quotation the following passage: 'Be brothers in the same race.' We will quote still another, which says, 'He who sees one part only of the Koran, and not the other, deserves misery in this life, and punishment in the other.'

"We see no motive for requiring a constitution or a national assembly, and we shall not in any manner admit such an institution. We have subdued the Christians, and conquered their territory, by the power of the sword; and we are unwilling to divide with them the administration of the country, and to let them participate in the direction of the affairs of the government.

"The equality of the Christians with the Turks has been decreed. This is a decree of the Sultan, — a decree the subject of which admits much discussion, into which we will nct go; but as to dividing the empire with the Christians, this cannot be done. We must peremptorily declare it.

"Other nations, as England, Russia, and France, do not permit their Mussulman, Tartar, Hindoo, and Arabic subjects to participate in the affairs of the government. What others do not do, and are not compelled to do, we should not do; and no person, nor any government in the world, can oblige us to do it." [1]

In the summer of 1875 an insurrection broke out in Herzegovina. For a time it was regarded as an insignificant affair; and, not being promptly attended to by the government, it spread rapidly, and received encouragement from abroad. On the request of the Turkish Government, the representatives of the great powers united in sending a commission into the disturbed district to inquire into abuses, and redress grievances. England joined in the plan with reluctance, and only upon the urgent solicitation of the Porte. Lord Derby thought it was better that the Turkish Government should rely on their own resources to suppress the insurrection, and should deal with it as a local outbreak, and not give it international importance by appealing to the support of the

---

[1] State Dept. Docs., 1877, p. 582.

treaty-powers. The efforts of the commission failed, because, as it was said, the insurgents had no faith in reforms promised by the Turks alone : what they wanted was European intervention to guarantee the reforms. This the Turkish Government would not assent to. In December, 1875, the government of Austria-Hungary, anxious to bring about a speedy settlement, in order to prevent its own subjects from being affected by the constantly-enlarging spirit of insubordination, proposed the following measures for pacification : —

1. Religious liberty, full and entire.

2. Abolition of the farming of taxes.

3. A law to guarantee that the direct taxation of Bosnia and the Herzegovina should be employed for the immediate interests of the provinces.

4. A special commission, composed of an equal number of Mussulmans and Christians, to superintend the execution of the reforms proclaimed and proposed.

5. The amelioration of the condition of the rural population.

The representatives of the six powers, under

instructions from their governments, supported these measures of reform ; but they came to nothing. The American ambassador in Turkey says, " My belief is, that the enlightened statesmen then in the imperial ministry saw clearly the evils out of which the insurrection had grown, and were sincere and determined in their efforts to reform them ; but the same two insurmountable difficulties confronted them, — the want of confidence in their promises, on the one hand, and the hostile Mussulman sentiment, on the other."[1]

After this failure, the representatives of Russia, Austria-Hungary, and Germany, met at Berlin on the 14th of May, 1876, and agreed upon a proposition known as the " Berlin Memorandum." It provided for a guaranty by the great powers of the several reforms already proclaimed, but not reduced to practice. Great Britain objected to the memorandum, and refused to sign it on the ground "that it must obviously and inevitably lead to the military occupation of Turkey."[2]

---

[1] State Dept. Docs., 1876–77, p. 581.

[2] Earl of Beaconsfield in House of Lords, Feb. 20, 1877.

Four days after the Berlin conference, the Emperor-king of Austria-Hungary stated, at an official reception, that "the events in the East have only strengthened my resolution, and that of the two great neighboring states, to draw more closely and intimately the relations which have already existed between our empires."

At this time the horrible atrocities which had been committed in Bulgaria during the first week in May had not been made public; and the details were not fully known until in August following. Mr. Eugene Schuyler, the American consul-general in Turkey, visited the insurrectionary district, and made a report on the 10th August, which more than confirmed the dark rumors which had prevailed for a few weeks previous. The outbreak against the Turkish authority was premature and insignificant. The insurgents made little or no resistance to the troops sent against them. In many instances they surrendered their arms upon the first demand. Nearly all the villages which were attacked by the bashi-bazouks were burned and pillaged, as were also all those which had been abandoned by the terrified inhabitants. The inhabitants of some villages were massacred after exhibitions of the most ferocious cruelty, and the violation, not only of women and girls, but even persons of the other sex. These crimes were committed by the regular troops as well as by the bashi-bazouks.

Commenting upon these disclosures, Mr. Gladstone says, "There is not a criminal in an European jail, there is not a cannibal in the South Sea Islands, whose indignation would not rise and overboil at the recital of that which has been done, which has too late been examined, but which remains unavenged; which has left behind all the foul and all the fierce passions that produced it, and which may again spring up, in another murderous harvest, from the soil soaked and reeking with blood, and in the air tainted with every imaginable deed of crime and shame. That such things should be done once is a damning disgrace to the portion of our race which did them; that a door should be left open for their ever-so-barely possible repetition would spread that shame over the whole."[1]

On the 2d July, 1876, the Prince of Servia and the Hospodar of Montenegro declared war against Turkey.

The position of the British Government at this time is found in a declaration made by the Earl of Derby, minister of foreign affairs, on the 14th July. He said, "We undertook, twenty years ago, to guarantee the Sick Man against murder; but we never undertook to guarantee him against suicide or sudden death. Now, that is, in a few words, our policy as regards this war now going on [i.e., between Servia, Montenegro, and Turkey]. We shall not intervene; but we shall do our utmost, if necessary, to discourage others from intervening."

When the English people became fully acquainted with the details of the Bulgarian atrocities, public feeling ran very high against the policy of adhering to the provisions of the Treaty of Paris, guaranteeing non-interference

[1] Bulgarian Horrors and the Question of the East. By W. E. Gladstone.

in the administration of the Turkish Government over its Christian subjects. The ministry began cautiously to change ground. Mr. Disraeli said in the House of Commons, on the 11th August, "Those who suppose that England ever would uphold, or at this moment is upholding, Turkey, from blind superstition, and from a want of sympathy with the highest aspirations of humanity, are deceived. What our duty is at this critical moment is to maintain the empire of England ; nor will we ever consent to any step, although it may obtain comparative quiet and a false prosperity, which could hazard the existence of this empire."

Under this bit of buncombe, this appeal to the "enlightened selfishness" of the British merchant, a change of front was about to take place. The speech from the throne a few days afterwards (15th August) stated, that, when a favorable opportunity presented itself, the government was ready to offer its good offices for the purpose of mediation between the contending parties. On the 21st September, the Earl of Derby sent a despatch to the British ambassador in Turkey, in which, after speaking of the just indignation which had been excited by the cruelties to the Bulgarian peasantry, he said, "No political considerations would justify the toleration of such acts; and one of the foremost conditions for the settlement of the questions now pending must be, that ample reparation shall be afforded to the sufferers, and their future security guaranteed."

About the same time, Mr. Gladstone published a pamphlet on "The Bulgarian Horrors and the Question of the East," which made a great stir in political circles. He denounced the policy of the British ministry, and urged that the government should intervene to bring about a termination of the war then going on, and should, in addition, aim at the accomplishment of these three objects; namely, —

"1. To put a stop to the anarchical misrule (let the phrase be excused), the plundering, the murdering, which, as we now seem to learn upon sufficient evidence, still desolate Bulgaria.

"2. To make effectual provision against the recurrence of the outrages recently perpetrated under the sanction of the Ottoman Government, by excluding its administrative action for the future, not only from Bosnia and the Herzegovina, but also, and above all, from Bulgaria ; upon which, at best, there will remain, for years and for generations, the traces of its foul and bloody hand.

" 3. To redeem by these measures the honor of the British name, which, in the deplorable events of the year, has been more gravely compromised than I have known it to be at any former period."

The anti-Turkish sentiment which Mr. Gladstone's vigorously-expressed views produced was strengthened by the publication, some time later, of Mr. Edward A. Freeman's article on the Turks in Europe. After answering the questions, Who is the Turk? what has he done in Europe? what is to be done with him? he concludes, " He came in as an alien and barbarian, encamped on the soil of Europe: at the end of five hundred years, he remains an alien and barbarian, encamped on soil which he has no more made his own than it was when he first took Kallipolis. His rule during all that time has been the rule of strangers over enslaved nations in their own land: it has been the rule of cruelty, faithlessness, and brutal lust: it has not been government, but organized brigandage. His rule cannot be reformed. While all other nations get better and better, the Turk gets worse and worse; and, when the chief powers of Europe join in demanding that he should make even the smallest reform, he impudently refuses to make any. If there was any thing to be said for him before the late conference, there is nothing to be said for him now. For an evil which cannot be reformed, there is one remedy only, — to get rid of it. Justice, reason, humanity, demand that the rule of the Turk in Europe should be got rid of; and the time for getting rid of it has now come."

On the 27th of September, the Lord Mayor of London and a deputation of citizens called on the Earl of Derby, and stated, that, at a meeting held on the 19th of that month (three days, it will be observed, before the earl sent his stiff despatch to the ambassador in Turkey), the feeling on the Turkish question was very strong indeed, "and went to show that the old foreign policy of England with regard to Turkey and the East was no longer tenable."

In order to open the way for a conference of the treaty-powers, England proposed an armistice of six weeks between Turkey and Servia. The Turkish Government proposed six months. The Russian Government demanded an immediate armistice of from four to six weeks, under penalty of breaking off diplomatic relations.

The Turkish Government complied with the demand; and the representatives of the treaty-powers, upon the suggestion of the British Government, soon after assembled at Constantinople to settle the conditions of peace. On the 2d of November, before the conference took place, the British ambassador in Russia had an interview with the Emperor Alexander, in which "His Majesty pledged his sacred word of honor, in the most earnest and solemn manner, that he had no intention of acquiring Constantinople, and that, if necessity should oblige him to occupy a portion of Bulgaria, it would only be provisionally, and until the peace and the safety of the Christian population were secured."

A few days later (10th November) the emperor made a speech at Moscow, in which he said, "I have striven, and shall still strive, to obtain a real improvement of the position of the Christians in the East by peaceful means." But, "should I see that we cannot obtain such guaranties as are necessary for carrying out what we have a right to demand of the Porte, I am firmly determined to act independently; and I am convinced, that, in this case, the whole of Russia will respond to my summons, should I consider it necessary, and should the honor of Russia require it."

The preliminary conference at Constantinople was opened on the 11th December, and was participated in by representatives from Great Britain, France, Russia, Austria-Hungary, Germany, and Italy. The purposes of that conference, and the failure to accomplish any satisfactory results, can be best understood by quoting from the speech of the Marquis of Salisbury, who was the chief representative, at the conference, on the part of Great Britain. Replying to an attack of the Duke of Argyll upon the policy of the government, the marquis said, —

"In the treaty of 1856 the intention of Turkey to reform herself was recognized in the most solemn manner; and each of the powers for itself — I am not now speaking of their mutual obligations — guaranteed in the most distinct manner the integrity and independence of the Ottoman Empire. That treaty was signed by the government of which the noble duke was a member.[1] But in the summer of 1875 a rebellion broke out. My noble friend (Lord Derby) spoke of not fostering that rebellion, and inviting sympathizers from outside to keep it up; and then he was denounced by the very men who signed the treaty of 1856 as though he had committed some great crime, not only against international law, but against morality. I admit how much events have modified the interpretation we are to put on the treaty of 1856; but that, at the beginning, blame should have been levelled against my noble friend for his efforts to maintain it by one of the ministers who gave that guaranty, was a very extraordinary circumstance. It soon became evident that the sanguine hopes of 1856 would not be realized, and that the exact attitude of this country towards Turkey could not remain as it was in 1856. But we were not bound, nor should we be justified in at once turning round on our ancient ally who had received encouragement from us so long, and who counted on our support. If the alliance was broken up, if our exertions for the maintenance of the Ottoman Empire were to cease, assuredly it was our part to struggle to the last against a

[1] The Duke of Argyll.

change which forced upon us a new and unexpected interpretation of a treaty by which our country was pledged; assuredly it was our duty to exhaust appeal, remonstrance, exhortation, before deserting a cause we had hitherto maintained ; and if we had taken any other course, however deep the guilt of the Turks, however low you may put their intelligence, they would have had fair ground of complaint against this country.   My right honorable friend in the other House had compared our change of policy to the change which a man makes who puts on a great-coat in winter, instead of wearing the same clothes as he did in summer. We had changed as far as events compelled us ; but we had not changed our traditional policy without hesitation and without sorrow ; and we still clung to the hope that some alteration would occur in the councils of Turkey, which would bring that alliance back to the same state as it was before.   Now, my lords, that was the explanation of the reason why we went into the conference, — distinctly not as a preliminary to force, but as a means of peaceful persuasion.   That being so, it necessarily followed, as the noble lord opposite remarked, that Russia was the motive-power of the conference.   That is not the way in which I should prefer to phrase it ; but at the same time I do not deny that it is absolutely true in a sense.   It is true that we went into the conference, first of all to restore peace between Turkey and Servia, and then to obtain a government for the Turkish Provinces ; but, undoubtedly, we also went to stop a great and menacing danger, namely, the prospect of a war between Russia and the Porte. This, then, being the evil which we came to avert, it naturally was in pointing out that evil that our moral influence on the Porte rested. We said to Turkey, 'Unless you do this or that, this terrible danger, which may well involve the loss of your empire, is ready to fall upon you. We hope that our influence and advice may be able to avert it ; indeed, we come here for that purpose : but we warn you that we shall accept no responsibility for the future, if you treat our advice with disdain.' Undoubtedly it was in this sense true that the fear of the result of a rupture of the congress — the fear of a breach with Russia — was the motive-force of the conference. It seems to me, as it must to everybody else, that the refusal of the Turks is a mystery ; for the infatuation of that course seems to be so tremendous."[1]

The Earl of Beaconsfield (Disraeli) also replied to the Duke of Argyll on the same occasion ; and, in the course of his speech, said, —

"There were two great policies before us with regard to the Christian subjects of the Porte. There was the Russian plan, deserving of all respect : it was a plan for establishing a chain of autonomous states tributary to the Porte, but in every other sense independent. No one can deny that was a large scheme, worthy of a statesman, and worthy of the deepest consideration. But the deepest considera-

[1] Speech in the House of Lords, 20th February, 1877.

tion that her Majesty's government could give to it was that they were forced entirely to disapprove of that scheme. This scheme of a chain of autonomous states in the Balkan country, and, indeed, in the whole of the country, that during the last half-century has been known as European Turkey, is a state of affairs that had existed before. The Turks did not step from Asia to conquer Constantinople, as is sometimes mentioned in the speeches at the national conferences. (A laugh.) It was very gradually that they entered into Europe. As a military power they obtained territories near the Black Sea, and ultimately entered into Thracia ; and there they remained with all these independent and autonomous states. There was, of course, an Emperor of Constantinople, there was a King of Bulgaria, there was a King of Servia, there was a Hospodar of Wallachia, there was a Duke of Athens, and there was a Prince of Corinth. And what happened ? The new military power that had entered into Europe gradually absorbed and conquered all these independent states ; and having conquered these independent states, these kingdoms and duchies, the Empire of Constantinople (being limited to its matchless city, and to what in modern language is called a cabbage-garden) was invested and fell. And it did occur to us, that if there were a chain of autonomous States, and the possessors of Constantinople were limited to a cabbage-garden, probably the same result might occur. Well, I do not pretend to say who first introduced this word ' autonomy' into these negotiations. If we did, we must bear the blame. But against this plan of the Russian court we proposed what was called by some one — the phrase was adopted at last — 'administrative autonomy; ' and we defined that administrative autonomy to be an institution that would secure the Christian subjects of the Porte some control over their own affairs, and some security from excesses of arbitrary power."

Referring, in conclusion, to the services of the Marquis of Salisbury at the conference, he said, " My noble friend fell only into one error, which I should have fallen into myself; and I believe every member of this House would have fallen into it. He gave too much credit to the Turks for common sense ; and he could not believe, that, when he made so admirable an arrangement in their favor, they would have lost so happy an opportunity."

In the mean time great changes had been taking place in the Turkish Government. On the 30th May, 1876, the Sultan, Abdul-Aziz, who had reigned since 1861, was deposed by the Grand Vizier, who was supported by the soldiers and the people. The nephew of the deposed Sultan succeeded to the throne as Murad V. On the 31st

of August, after a reign of three months, Sultan
Murad V. was deposed by the council of ministers, on the ground of mental incapacity ; and his
brother was proclaimed Sultan under the title of
Abdul-Hamid II.

The despatch of the American ambassador in
Turkey, dated 1st September, 1876, throws some
light on this revolutionary proceeding. He men-
tions a prediction which he had made previous to
the deposition of Abdul-Aziz, namely, that the
Sultan and his nephew, the then heir-apparent,
had provoked their destiny by visiting the Paris
Exposition of 1867, and setting foot on Christian
soil, and then says, —

"When the revolution broke out which de-
throned Abdul-Aziz, I could not resist the convic-
tion that it would be completed only by the
elevation of Hamid. Every thing which occurred
subsequently only strengthened it. Murad was
placed on the throne temporarily, because he was
the next in the line of the succession, and to
meet in public estimation the requirements of the
Moslem law, but with no intention that he should
enjoy more than a temporary occupation." [1]

[1] State Dept. Docs., 1876–77, p. 583.

On the 7th September, the new Sultan was invested with the sword of Othman,[1] and issued an address, in which he said, —

" The great object to be aimed at is to adopt measures for placing the laws and regulations of the country upon bases which shall inspire confidence in their execution. For this purpose, it is indispensable to proceed to the establishment of a general council or national assembly (the original Turkish expression is *medjiliss oumoumi*), whose acts will inspire every confidence in the nation, and will be in harmony with the customs, aptitudes, and capabilities of the populations of the empire. The mission and duty of this council will be to guarantee, without exception, the faithful execution of the existing laws, or of those which shall be promulgated in conformity with the provisions of the *sheri,* in connection with the real and legitimate wants of the country and its inhabitants, as also to control the equilibrium of the revenue, and expenditures of the empire." [2]

In accordance with this recommendation, the

---

[1] No such investiture was made in the case of Murad V.

[2] From Daily Levant Herald, Sept. 12, 1876.

council of ministers prepared a constitution for
the Ottoman Empire, providing for the establishment of representative institutions. On the 23d
December, the constitution was promulgated ;
and a parliament was called to assemble on the
13th March following, and actually assembled on
the 19th.

In this connection, the speech made by a member of the parliament — a rough-looking representative from Kurdistan — will be of interest, as
showing the sentiments of the common people on
the question of foreign interference.   In reply to
some remarks about the great misery brought
about by the present state of things, he said, —

"You talk of misery ; and yet I see brilliant
uniforms, luxurious palaces, and many elegant
carriages, in Constantinople. Come to our province, if you really want to know what misery
means. I myself, like most of the people in my
province, go about in rags ; and it was only by a
great effort and sacrifice that I have been able to
get this coat to appear decently among you ; and
still I am ready to give up this coat, and resume
my old rags, in order to fight for the existence and

honor of my country. No one has a right to interfere with our own domestic affairs ; and we Ottomans protest solemnly against such interference by any foreign power." [1]

.

After the failure of the conference at Constantinople, Prince Gortschakoff issued a circular, in which, after reciting what had taken place, he said, " It is necessary for us to know what the cabinets, with which we have hitherto acted in common, propose to do, with a view of meeting this refusal, and insuring the execution of their wishes."

But, before any response had been made to this request for information, the Russian Government, fearing that it might be embarrassed if the other governments should not agree, prepared a protocol, which, after some verbal amendments, was signed by the representatives of the six powers, at London, on the 31st March, 1877. After taking cognizance of the peace which had recently been concluded between

[1] Vienna Correspondent London Times, April 4, 1877.

Turkey and Servia, and taking cognizance, also, of the good intentions of the Porte, as shown in its declarations made from time to time during the past year, the protocol invites the Porte to place its army on a peace-footing, and then declares, that "the powers propose to watch carefully, by means of their representatives at Constantinople, and their local agents, the manner in which the promises of the Ottoman Government are carried into effect.

"If their hopes should once more be disappointed, and if the condition of the Christian subjects of the Sultan should not be improved in a manner to prevent the return of the complications which periodically disturb the peace of the East, they think it right to declare that such a state of affairs would be incompatible with their interests, and those of Europe in general. In such case, they reserve to themselves to consider in common as to the means which they may deem best fitted to secure the well-being of the Christian populations, and the interests of the general peace."

On affixing his signature, the Russian ambassador filed the following declaration : —

" If peace with Montenegro is concluded, and the Porte accepts the advice of Europe, and shows itself ready to replace its forces on a peace-footing, and seriously to undertake the reforms mentioned in the protocol, let it send to St. Petersburg a special envoy to treat of disarmament, to which his Majesty the Emperor would also, on his part, consent.

" If massacres similar to those which have stained Bulgaria with blood take place, this would necessarily put a stop to the measures of demobilization."

If Turkey had been desirous of peace, there could have been no hesitation in giving its assent to this indeterminate declaration. But the war-party evidently had the ascendency in the councils of the divan ; and the protocol was rejected. A counter-declaration was made, in which the signatory powers were notified (1) that, adopting toward Montenegro the same line of conduct which brought about the pacification of Servia, the Sublime Porte spontaneously informed the prince two months ago that it would spare no effort to arrive at an understanding with him,

even at the price of certain sacrifices; (2) that
the Imperial Government was prepared to apply
all the promised reforms; but those reforms, in
conformity with the fundamental provisions of
the constitution, could not have a special or exclusive character, and it was in that spirit that
the Imperial Government, in its full and entire
liberty, would continue to apply its instructions;
(3) that Turkey was ready to place its armies on
a peace-footing as soon as it saw the Russian
Government take measures to the same end; (4)
with regard to the disturbances which might
break out in Turkey, and stop the demobilization
of the Russian army, the Turkish Government
repelled the injurious terms in which the idea
had been expressed, and stated its belief that
Europe was convinced that the recent disturbances were due to foreign instigation, i.e.,
Russia's; (5) concerning the despatch of the
special envoy to St. Petersburg to treat on the
question of disarmament, the Imperial Government, which would have no reason to refuse an
act of courtesy reciprocally required by diplomatic usages, perceives no connection between

that act of international courtesy and the disarmament which there was no plausible motive for delaying, and which might be carried into effect by a single telegraphic order.

In conclusion it was declared, that, "maintaining with other friendly states relations regulated by international law and treaties, Turkey cannot allow foreign agents or representatives, charged to protect the interests of their compatriots, to have any mission of official supervision. The Imperial Government, in fact, is not aware how it can have deserved so ill of justice and civilization as to see itself placed in a humiliating position without example in the world.[1] The Treaty of Paris gave an explicit sanction to the principle of non-intervention. This treaty, which binds together the powers who participated in it, as well as Turkey, cannot be abolished by a protocol in which Turkey has had no share ; and, if Turkey appeals to the stipulations of the Treaty of Paris, it is not that that treaty has created in her favor any rights which she would not possess without it, but rather for the purpose of calling

[1] This after the horrors of Bulgaria.

attention to grave reasons, which, in interest of the general peace of Europe, induced the powers twenty years ago to place the recognition of the inviolability of this empire's right to sovereignty under guaranty of collective promise."

When the Turkish ambassador in London called upon the Earl of Derby, on the 12th of April, to deliver the above circular, the British minister of foreign affairs expressed his deep regrets at the view the Porte had taken, and said he could not see what further steps England could take to avert the war which appeared to be inevitable.

On the 24th April (N. S.) the Tsar, who was at Kicheneff with the army, issued his manifesto, in which he said, —

"For two years we have made incessant efforts to induce the Porte to effect such reforms as would protect the Christians in Bosnia, Herzegovina, and Bulgaria, from the arbitrary measures of the local authorities. The accomplishment of these reforms was absolutely stipulated by anterior engagements contracted by the Porte toward the whole of Europe. Our efforts, supported by diplomatic representations made in common by the other governments, have not, however, attained their object. The Porte has remained unshaken in its formal refusal of any effective guaranty for the security of its Christian subjects, and has rejected the conclusions of the Constantinople conference. Wishing to essay every possible means of conciliation in order to persuade the Porte, we proposed to the other cabinets to draw up a special protocol, comprising the most essential conditions of the Constantinople conference, and to invite the Turkish Government to adhere to this international act, which states the extreme limits of our peaceful demands. But our expectation was not fulfilled. The Porte did not defer to this unanimous wish of Christian Europe, and did not adhere to the conclusions of the protocol. Having exhausted pacific efforts, we are compelled, by the haughty obstinacy of the Porte, to proceed to more decisive acts, feeling that equity and our own dignity enjoin it. By her refusal, Turkey places us under the necessity of having recourse to arms. Profoundly convinced

of the justice of our cause, and humbly com-
mitting ourselves to the grace and help of the
Most High, we make known to our faithful subjects that the moment foreseen, when we pro-
nounced words to which all Russia responded
with complete unanimity, has now arrived. We
expressed the intention to act independently
when we deemed it necessary, and when Russia's
honor should demand it. And now, invoking
the blessing of God upon our valiant armies,
we give them the order to cross the Turkish
frontier."

On the same day, the telegraph announced
that fifty thousand Russians crossed the Pruth
at Jassy, Kabul, and Bolgrad.

W 88

THE RUSSIAN GOVERNMENT.

EMPEROR, ALEXANDER II. NICOLAÏÉVITCH, born the 17th April, 1818, succeeded his father (Nicholas I. Pavlovitch) the 18th of February, 1855. His children are, (1) *Alexander*-Alexandrovitch, Hereditary Grand Duke, born 26th February, 1845, commandant of the Imperial Guard, general of infantry and cavalry; (2) *Vladimir*-Alexandrovitch, Grand Duke, born 10th April, 1847, lieutenant-general, commanding first division of Imperial Guards; (3) *Alexis*-Alexandrovitch, Grand Duke, born 2d January, 1850, colonel, and aide-de-camp of the emperor; (4) *Marie*-Alexandrovna, Grand Duchesse, born 5th October, 1853; (5) *Sergius*-Alexandrovitch, Grand Duke, born 29th April, 1857, chief of the second

---

[1] The statements in relation to the governments and industries of Russia and Turkey are collated from Martin's Statesman's Year-Book for 1877, the Almanach de Gotha for 1877, and the United States Report on Commercial Relations, 1875.

battalion of Chasseurs of the Guard ; (6) *Paul-*
Alexandrovitch, Grand Duke, born 3d October,
1860, chief of the Koura Regiment.

The government of Russia is an absolute hereditary monarchy. The administration of the
empire is intrusted to four colleges, or boards of
government. (1.) The *Council of the Empire*,
which consists of certain officials, and such other
persons as the emperor may from time to time
appoint. In 1875 the council contained forty-
two members specially appointed by the emperor.
The Grand Duke Constantine is the president ;
the hereditary Grand Duke Alexander is a member ; and all the ministries are members *ex officio.*
It is intrusted by law or custom with many
important functions, such as examining and criti-
cising the annual budget, declaring war, and con-
cluding peace ; but the emperor is not bound by
its decisions. (2.) The *Senate*, which was origi-
nally intrusted with the supreme power during
the absence or minority of the monarch, and was
intended to exercise a controlling influence in all
sections of the administration. It is now re-
stricted to judicial matters, and is little more than

a Supreme Court of Appeal.[1] (3.) The *Committee of Ministers*, which is presided over by Gen. Ignatieff, and which includes the heads of the different departments, ten in number ; namely, Foreign Affairs, War, Navy, Interior, Public Instruction, Finance, Justice, Imperial Domains, Public Works and Railways, Imperial Court. (4.) The *Holy Synod*, which has the superintendence of the religious affairs of the empire : it is presided over by Isidore, the Metropolitan of Novgorod.

For the purposes of territorial administration, European Russia, exclusive of Poland, the Baltic Provinces, Finland, and the Caucasus, each of which has a peculiar administration of its own, is divided into forty-six provinces (*guberanii*) ; and each province is subdivided into districts (*uyezdi*).

According to enumerations made by the government during the years 1870 to 1873, the total population of the empire numbers 85,685,945, averaging ten to the square mile. The total population of Russia Proper (in Europe) is 65,-504,659 ; of European Russia, 78,281,447.

1 Wallace's Russia.

The estimated revenue for 1876 was £81,448,-329; expenditures, £79,443,630. The estimated amount of the entire public debt on the 1st January, 1876, was £250,962,000, of which £183,-091,000 was bearing interest, and £77,871,000 was not bearing interest. The amount of bank-notes in circulation (a forced currency) on the 1st January, 1876, was £113,044,783.

The military forces of the empire in time of war are stated as follows : Russia in Europe (troops in the field), officers, 18,150 ; combatants, 674,957 ; non-combatants, 53,042 ; cannons, 2,172 ; horses, 132,550. Total force in Europe, including troops in the field, in station, and in reserve : officers, 38,200 ; combatants, 1,358,557 ; non-combatants, 142,742 ; horses, 171,350. In the Caucasus, officers, 4,906 ; combatants, 216,-380; non-combatants, 19,131 ; horses, 21,040. In Asia, officers, 1,057 ; combatants, 34,700 ; non-combatants, 4,000 ; horses, 3,500.

The strength of the navy was officially returned in March, 1876, as follows : 89 admirals, 1,357 officers, 540 pilots, 215 officers of artillery, 150 naval constructors, 554 master mechanics, 58 official architects, 291 surgeons, 331 admiralty officers, and 504 civil functionaries. The total number of men required to man the fleets is 25,943. The Baltic fleet consists of 27 ironclads carrying 197 guns, 44 armed steamers carrying 190 guns, and 66 steam transports. The Black-sea fleet consists of 2 ironclads, 25 armed steamers, and 4 transports. The fleet in the Caspian Sea consists of 11 armed steamers and 8 steamers not armed. The Siberian fleet consists of 9 armed steamers and 18 steamers not armed. In the Sea of Aral there are 6 steamers. In the White Sea there are 3 steamers. The total number of Russian war-vessels is 223; number of guns, 561; tonnage, 188,120; horse-power, 31,080. The most powerful vessel is the mast-less turret ship, "Peter the Great," launched at Cronstadt in 1874. This ship has two turrets armed with four thirty-five-ton guns made by Krupp. The ironclad fleet includes 29 vessels with 184 guns, 9,210 horse-power, and of 74,793 tons burden. It is admitted that the Russian fleet in the Black Sea is utterly unable to cope with the Turkish fleet.

TRADE AND NAVIGATION.

The following statement, taken from the last government report on commercial relations (1875), shows the trade between Russia and other portions of Europe and the United States in 1874 :—

	Export.	Import.	Total Trade.
	Silver rubles.	*Silver rubles.*	*Silver rubles*[1]
Great Britain...........	136,461,698	126,263,853	262,725,551
Germany...............	136,466,850	174,729,769	311,196,619
France...............	33,056,382	19,728,941	52,785,323
Austria	33,414,979	20,706,710	54,121,689
Italy.................	8,696,999	10,984,200	19,681,199
Holland and Belgium....	28,628,349	14,997,238	43,625,587
Sweden and Norway.....	10,920,953	3,301,982	14,222,935
Denmark..............	6,601,372	194,446	6,795,818
Turkey, Greece, and Rou-mania...............	14,060,603	16,527,287	30,587,890
United States..........	1,810,780	39,410,552	41,221,332
Finland...............	9,028,841	10,648,411	19,677,252
All other States........	1,370,523	10,640,399	12,010,912
Total...............	421,508,329	447,596,388	869,104,717

The principal articles of export in 1874 from Russia to Europe and America were as follows :—

[1] The silver ruble represents seventy-five cents in American currency.

	Silver rubles.
Grain and legumes	212,298,906
Cattle and sheep	7,664,906
Horses	2,135,373
Wool	11,526,271
Tallow	2,695,992
Bristles	3,101,906
Horse manes and tails	801,734
Feathers and downs	1,029,714
Bones	1,241,722
Hides	2,207,747
Tobacco in leaves, cut, cigars	1,260,642
Flax and flax tow	53,965,206
Flax and hemp seed	25,673,139
Hemp	15,150,564
Wood	29,596,636
Resin	1,003,259
Bolt rope, cordage, sail-cloth	1,781,507
Crash	81,980
Linen	683,851
Malachite goods	77,170
Furs	1,535,616
Leather	1,103,873
Sheet iron	1,878,778
Crude iron	1,052,009
Caviaes	1,005,315
Isinglass	1,383,302
Rags	437,749
Miscellaneous	20,104,621
Total	411,489,588
Amounts for Finland added	9,028,841
Grand total for Europe and America	420,518,329

The total export of grain from the Russian Empire from 1860 to Aug, 1. 1875, reduced to American bushels and gold dollars, was as follows : —

	Bushels.	Gold dollars.
1860............................	51,055,855	47,564,433
1865............................	56,977,580	50,555,960
1870............................	124,683,283	129,907,389
1871............................	143,524,283	144,865,826
1872............................	96,131,581	104,578,224
1873............................	127,584,529	133,974,648
1874............................	161,854,548	158,476,691
1875 to Aug. 1..................	68,985,640	72,173,799

The number of Russian ships engaged in foreign trade in 1874 was 621 ; number in coasting trade bearing Russian flag, 1,672 ; number of steamers on rivers and lakes of the empire, 385.

The length of railways open for traffic in European Russia in 1875 was 11,591 miles, and nearly 6,000 miles of additional road were projected. The length of telegraph-lines was 31,459 miles.

THE TURKISH GOVERNMENT.

SULTAN, ABDUL-HAMID II., born 5th September, 1842, succeeded to power 31st August, 1876. He is the son of Sultan Abdul-Medjid, and is the thirty-fifth in male descent from the house of Othman, the founder of the empire.

The Grand Vizier, whose functions were defined in the year 132 of the Hegira, or 754 years after the Christian Era, is the supreme chief of the temporal administration. The Sheik-ul-Islam, or Ancient of Islam, is the head of the church. Both these officers are appointed by the Sultan. The Koran has heretofore been the only recognized source of civil and religious law. Whether the new legislative body which has recently been assembled under the charter promulgated Dec. 23, 1876, has authority to make any laws inconsistent with the teachings of the Koran, does not appear. The divan, or ministerial council, is divided into eight departments, or bureaus, — War, Finance, Marine, Commerce, Public Works,

Police, Justice, and Public Instruction. There have been constant changes of ministers in recent years, the average term of service of members of the divan not exceeding four months. The empire is divided into districts of three classes, — the " Vilayet," the highest, the " Sanjak," a subdivision, and the " Caza," the unit of the political organization. This division is copied from the French system, and corresponds to the Provinces, Prefectures, and Sous-prefectures in that country.

The following table gives the population of the several divisions of the highest class, and the number of Mahometans in each, estimated in 1876 : —

Vilayets.	Population.	Mahometans.	Christians and Israelites.
Constantinople [1]	327,750	183,540	144,210
Adrianople	1,354,567	523,009	831,558
Danube	1,994,821	819,226	1,175,527
Salonica	1,028,141	429,410	598,731
Janina	711,250	250,649	460,601
Roumelia	1,168,016	617,479	550,537
Bosnia	1,357,984	493,148	864,836
Crete	200,000	38,000	162,000
Total [2]	8,232,461	3,444,461	4,788,000

[1] This includes only the European part of the city.

[2] Exclusive of about 82,000 in the army, all of whom are Mahometans.

This statement includes only that portion of Turkey in Europe over which the Turkish Government exercises immediate rule.

The total revenue of the government, including the payments of the tributary states amounted, in 1875–76, to £19,106,352 : the expenditures for the same year amounted to £23,143,276. There has been an annual deficit dating back to the year 1850. In 1875 the foreign debt, contracted during the preceding twenty years, amounted to £184,981,783 ; and the internal and floating debt was estimated at from nine millions to thirty millions of pounds. The government failed to pay the interest on the public debt last year ; and an order of the government announced that "no payments would be made until the internal affairs of the empire had become more settled." An issue of paper money was made 27th July, 1876, to what extent is not known.

The military forces were estimated in 1876 as follows (war footing) : infantry, 117,360 ; cavalry, 22,416 ; field artillery, 7,800 ; artillery in fortresses, 5,200 ; engineers, 1,600 ; detached corps, 16,000 ; total, 170,376. Reserves, 148,680 ; irregulars, 87,000 ; auxiliaries, 75,000. Non-Mussulmans are not liable to military service ; but they pay a tax on account of their exemption. The whole population of Turkey, including Asia and Africa, is variously estimated at from 28,000,000, to 48,000,000, of which 16,000,000 are said to be Mahometans. Of these, about 3,000,000 are included in the nomad tribes, not subject to conscription. Constantinople is also exempt from the conscription ; so that the population from which the Turkish army is to be recruited amounts to about 12,000,000.

The Turkish fleet contains twenty iron-clad ships, namely, seven frigates, eight corvettes, and five gunboats, and seventy other steamers, namely, five ships-of-the-line, five frigates, fifteen corvettes, and fifty-five despatch and gun boats. Most of the iron-clads were built in England. The two largest, " The Mésondivé " and " The Mendouhiyé," are each of nine thousand tons burden, twelve hundred and fifty horse-power, and carry twelve guns for 400-pound shot, three guns for 150-pound shot, and six guns for 20-pound shot.

TRADE AND NAVIGATION.

The number of vessels entered and cleared at the port of Constantinople during the year ending Dec. 31, 1874, was, steamers, 4,185 ; sailing-vessels, 16,489 ; total tonnage, 4,606,195. In 1865 the numbers were, steamers, 2,076 ; sailing-vessels, 14,885 ; tonnage, 4,244,948. A comparison of the tonnage carried respectively in steamers and sailing-vessels in 1865 and 1874 shows that the relation between numbers and tonnage has entirely changed within the last ten years here as everywhere else. In 1865 the 14,885 sailing-vessels carried 3,264,620 tons ; in 1874 the 16,489 sailing-vessels carried only 1,840,364 tons. In 1865 the 2,076 steamers carried only 914,320 tons : whereas in 1874 the 4,185 steamers carried 2,525,776 tons. Twenty-two per cent of the shipping is British.

The average annual value of goods imported into Turkey is estimated at $100,000,000, and the exports at about half that sum. There are no *official* returns of the foreign commerce. The principal import is of manufactured cotton goods from England, amounting in 1875 to £4,646,343.

Iron is imported mainly from Belgium ; corn and flour, from Odessa; sugar, from Egypt; coal, from England; petroleum, from the United States. The principal exports are wools, seeds, skins, and opium. The principal article exported to the United States is attar of roses.

The railways in European Turkey are ' the Varna-Rustchuk, 138½ miles ; Kuslendji-Ichernavoda, 40 miles ; Constantinople-Ballova, 350 miles ; Demotica-Dede-Agatoh, 61 miles; Irnova-Yambola, 66 miles ; Banialuka-Doberlin, 64 miles ; Salonica-Mitroritza, 225 miles. Total, 944½ miles. In Asiatic Turkey: Smyrna-Aïdin, 82½ miles ; Smyrna-Alashéïr, 82 miles; Haïdar Pacha (Scutari)-Ismidt, 56 miles. Total, 220½ miles.

The total length of telegraph-lines is 17,618 miles; and the length of wires, 31,230 miles.

TRIBUTARIES OF TURKEY IN EUROPE.

ROUMANIA, formerly Wallachia and Moldavia. Ruler: Prince Karl I., son of the late Prince Karl of Hohenzollern-Sigmaringen. He was elected as Prince of Roumania 10th May, 1866, and recognized by the Turkish Government 11th July, 1866. The constitution now in force was prepared by an assembly elected by universal suffrage in 1866. The legislative power is vested in a Senate and a Chamber of Deputies. The executive power is in the hands of the Prince, assisted by a council of five ministers, namely, of Foreign Affairs, the Interior, of War, of Finance, and of Justice. The revenue amounts to about $19,-000,000 per annum ; the expenditures, to a little more.

The effective force of the territorial army included, in 1876, 22,463 infantry and 12,184 cavalry. The population is estimated at about 4,000,000.

The staple article of export to Great Britain is corn, amounting, in 1875, to £569,990. Manufactured cotton goods of the value of £677,489 were imported from great Britain in the same year.

SERVIA: Ruler, Milan IV. Obrenovitch ; born 1855 ; proclaimed in 1868 ; crowned, 1872. He was elected by the National Assembly of Servia to succeed his uncle, who was assassinated in 1868. The executive power of the government is vested in the prince, assisted by a council of five ministers. The legislative authority is vested in the Senate and the Skoupchtina, or House of Representatives. The estimates of 1875–76 place the revenue at £705,134, and the expenditures at £696,137. The population by census of 1874 is 1,352,522. The standing army consists of 4,000 men. The national militia includes 70,000 men. The foreign trade is confined to Austria, Turkey, and Roumania.

TREATIES

BETWEEN RUSSIA AND THE UNITED STATES.

On the 17th April, 1824, a convention was concluded at St. Petersburg, between the United States and Russia, relative to navigation and fisheries of the Pacific. A provision in the treaty concerning establishments on the north-west coast of America was modified by the convention of 1867. (See p. 664, " Public Treaties.")

On the 18th December, 1832, a treaty of commerce was concluded at St. Petersburg. Art. I. provides for a reciprocal liberty of commerce and navigation between the two countries; Art. II., that vessels shall be upon an equal footing; Art. III. provides for equality of duties on imports; Art. IV. defines the applicability of the stipulations to vessels of both countries; Art. V. provides for equality in exportations; Art. VI. provides for equality of duties on produce of

either country, and for equality of prohibitions;
Art. VII. provides that Arts. II. to VI. inclu-
sive shall not be applicable to coastwise navigation; Art. VIII. provides for consular officers,
with privileges and powers of the most favored
nations, and with rights to settle certain disputes
between masters and crews; Art. IX. relates to
deserters from ships-of-war and merchant-vessels;
Art. X. relates to disposal and inheritance of
personal property; Art. XI provides that favors
granted to other nations shall become common
(" Public Treaties," pp. 666–669).

On the 22d July, 1854, a convention was concluded at Washington relative to the rights of
neutrals at sea. Art. I. declares that the two
high contracting parties recognize as permanent
and immutable the following principles; to wit,
1st, That free ships make free goods, that is to
say, that the effects or goods belonging to subjects or citizens of a power or state at war are
free from capture and confiscation when found
on board of neutral vessels, with the exception
of articles contraband of war; 2d, That the property of neutrals on board an enemy's vessel is

not subject to confiscation, unless the same be contraband of war. They engage to apply these principles to the commerce and navigation of all such states and powers as shall consent to adopt them on their part as permanent and immutable. Art. II. declares that the two parties reserve themselves to come to an ulterior understanding, as circumstances may require, with regard to the application and extension of the principles laid down in the first article. Art. III. provides that other nations acceding to the principles of the first article shall enjoy the same rights as the two contracting parties ("Public Treaties," pp. 670–671).

On the 30th March, 1867, a convention was concluded at Washington for the cession of the Russian Possessions in North America to the United States ("Public Treaties, pp. 671–673).

On the 27th January, 1868, a treaty was concluded at Washington, supplementary to the treaty of commerce and navigation, providing for the protection of trade-marks, and designating the places where the same should be deposited ("Public Treaties," p. 674).

TURKEY AND THE UNITED STATES.

A treaty of commerce and navigation between the United States and the Ottoman Empire was concluded 7th of May, 1830. Art. I. provides, that the merchants of the two countries shall have in either country the rights and privileges of the most favored nations. Art. II. provides for the establishment of consular officers in the two countries. Arts. III. and IV. relate to American vessels, the settlement of disputes, and the Turkish jurisdiction over American citizens. Art. V. provides that American vessels shall not take the flag of other powers, nor shall they grant their flag to vessels of other nations. Art. VI. provides for the exchange of courtesies between vessels-of-war. Art. VII. provides that merchant-vessels of the United States shall have the same liberty as vessels of the most favored nations in passing the Canal of the Imperial Residence, and going and coming in the Black Sea. Art. VIII. provides that merchant-ships shall not be impressed. Art. IX. relates to wrecks ("Public Treaties," pp. 583–585).

On the 25th February, 1862, an additional

treaty of commerce and navigation was concluded at Constantinople. Art. I. confirms the
privileges of citizens of the United States in the
Ottoman dominions, and provides that all rights,
privileges, and immunities granted to other
powers shall be equally granted to and exer-
cised and enjoyed by the citizens, vessels, commerce, and navigation of the United States.
Art. II. relates to the purchase of goods in the
Ottoman Empire, by United-States citizens. Art.
III. provides that citizens of the United States
engaging in trade within the Turkish dominions
shall be placed on the same footing as the
most favored class of Ottoman subjects. Art.
IV. provides for equality of duties on exports, equality of prohibitions, and the limitation of export duty in the Ottoman dominions.
Art. V. provides for equality of duties on imports, and the limitation of import duties in the
Ottoman dominions. Art. VI. provides that articles carried through the empire for importation
into Moldo-Wallachia and Servia shall not pay
duties until they reach those principalities.
Art. VII. relates to warehousing, bounties, &c.

Art. VIII. provides that vessels of the two countries shall have equal rights in the importation of goods. Art. IX. relates to tonnage duties. Art. X. defines the nationality of vessels. Art. XI. provides for the free passage of the Dardanelles. Art. XII. regulates the transit duty on articles carried through the Ottoman Empire. Art. XIII. defines the privileges of American traders in Turkey. Art. XIV. provides that tobacco and salt shall not be included among the articles which citizens of the United States are permitted to import into Turkey. Art. XV. reserves to the Sublime Porte the right of issuing a general prohibition against the importation of gunpowder, cannon, arms of war, or military stores ; but such prohibition will not come into operation until it shall have been officially notified. The other articles are not of general interest. (See "Public Treaties," pp. 585–591.)

INTERNATIONAL RULES FOR THE GOVERNMENT OF NEUTRALS.

THE treaty of Washington, signed on the 8th May, 1871, provided that the arbitrators appointed to settle the Alabama claims, so called, should, in deciding the matters submitted to them, be governed by the following rules, and by such principles of international law not inconsistent therewith, as the arbitrators should determine to have been applicable to the case. Rules : A neutral government is bound : First, to use due diligence to prevent the fitting-out, arming, or equipping, within its jurisdiction, of any vessel which it has reasonable ground to believe is intended to cruise, or to carry on war, against a power with which it is at peace, and also to use like diligence to prevent the departure from its jurisdiction of any vessel intended to cruise, or carry on war, as above; such vessel having been specially adapted, in whole or in part, within such jurisdiction, to warlike use; secondly, not to permit or suffer either belligerent to make use of its ports or waters as the base of naval operations against the other, or for the purpose of the renewal or augmentation of military supplies or arms, or the recruitment of men; thirdly, to exercise due diligence in its own ports and waters, and, as to all persons within its jurisdiction, to prevent any violation of the foregoing obligations and duties. ("Annual Register," 1871).

RUSSIAN LEGATION IN THE UNITED STATES.

Mr. Nicolas Shiskin, *Envoy Extraordinary and Minister Plenipotentiary.*

Mr. Grégoire de Willamov, *Secretary of Legation.*

UNITED STATES LEGATION IN RUSSIA.

Mr. George H. Boker, *Envoy Extraordinary and Minister Plenipotentiary.*

Mr. Hoffman Atkinson, *Secretary of Legation.*

TURKISH LEGATION IN THE UNITED STATES.

Gregoire Aristarchi Bey, *Envoy Extraordinary and Minister Plenipotentiary.*

Baltazzi Effendi, *Secretary of Legation.*

UNITED STATES LEGATION IN TURKEY.

Hon. Horace Maynard, *Minister Resident.*

Mr. Eugene Schuyler, *Secretary of Legation.*

www.ingramcontent.com/pod-product-compliance
Lightning Source LLC
Chambersburg PA
CBHW020337090426
42735CB00009B/1571